Making Fast Cash in a Down Economy Without Computer Skills

Diana Loera

NOTE -

While I hope that you are successful using one or more of these ideas, each person's experience is unique. You should also check your city's ordinances before implementing any of these ideas that may require permits, licenses or insurance.

I strive to keep my publishing costs as low as possible. Adding color photos to my books drive the book cost up considerably.

In my recipe books I add color photos. I did not add any photos to this book as being blunt, I wanted to save you money and also I think the ideas are ones that do not require illustrations for readers to grasp. Thank you for understanding.

Table of Contents

12 Extra Special Summer Dessert Fondue Recipes http://tinyurl.com/q7gpgw8

14 Extra Special Winter Holidays Fondue Recipes http://tinyurl.com/lkebggx

Awesome Thanksgiving Leftovers Revive Guide http://tinyurl.com/prxjayg

Best 100 Calorie or Less Dessert Recipes http://tinyurl.com/pn5b46c

Best Bacon Infused Dessert Recipes: 20 Mouthwatering Delicious Desserts Infused with Bacon http://tinyurl.com/owxo3pl

Coca Cola Ham, Coca Cola Cake and Other Coca Cola Recipes http://tinyurl.com/pp2wvhz

Party Time Chicken Wing Recipes   http://tinyurl.com/ohsc9x8

Summertime Sangria   http://tinyurl.com/oxnlnhm

Best Bacon Infused Dessert Recipes http://tinyurl.com/q38aaox

Best Copycat Recipes on the Planet http://tinyurl.com/pcuj24q

Best Pumpkin Recipe http://tinyurl.com/oxdr8fq

Best West Virginia Recipes http://tinyurl.com/oqywpbq

Best Pumpkin Drink & Dessert Recipes http://tinyurl.com/nmwx3mb

Please visit www.LoeraPublishingLLC.com to see our complete selection of books. Topics include cooking, travel, recipes, how to, non- fiction and more.

Before we begin, please note that this book, as well as almost all of the books that I have published is created as an 8 ½ x 11 size softcover book.

I hate squinting at small print and didn't think it was fair to ask you to do so either. So all of my books are a large size for reading ease. Each one of my pages is equal to 3 or 4 pages in a normal sized book.

Anyway, with that being said – onward to information about this book.

In this crazy economy, more and more people are looking for ways to generate cash – as fast as possible.

I know several people, and you probably do too, who have filled out job application after job application and still are looking for work.

You may have been one of those people who has filled out application after application and not heard a word back.

You may have a friend or loved one who is desperately looking for work and nothing is panning out.

You may be worrying how you'll afford Christmas gifts, pay your child's tuition, put gas in your car or how you'll afford to pay your heating bills this winter.

When the economy was tanking and it was evident it wasn't turning around, I tested several ideas to generate income – without having to use a computer.

I then outlined my success in two books – one on scrapping and one on flea market selling.

I then spoke with quite a few people, especially those who found out that I had successful made money – fast – with scrapping and flea market selling who asked me if I had any other ideas that would be helpful to make cash fast.

I then starting writing an overview of the top money making ideas and this is the book that contains that information.

This book gives you an overview of ideas that have been proven to work for me or for someone I personally know.

I also included an overview of scrapping and flea market selling as both are fast cash makers.

The descriptions are not lengthy as this isn't a how to book.

It is a book that was designed to jump start your brain fast, cut to the chase and help you hit the ground running to generate a cash flow.

The idea behind this book is that there are ways to generate an income or supplement an income.

Like any job though, you do need to commit to making it work and treating it like a job.

Some of the options in this book do require a bit of cash, a vehicle, know how or other needs but in many cases, you may already have access at home to needed materials or have someone who is willing to help you.

Some of these ideas may generate more cash than others and some may generate cash much faster.

The main thing is that there are options to make money.

Some of these ideas may be ones you have thought about before. I do urge you to take a second look if that is the case. Times change, the economy changes and when you need ways to make cash – well, I look again at many ideas. You never know what might be the goose that lays the golden egg for you.

In my case, I had looked at one of the money making ideas in this book well over 20 years ago. The economy was very good then and I dismissed the idea and moved on.

I again looked at the idea about five years ago and my husband wasn't overly interested so I again passed it by.

Last year I decided we really needed to give it a go and thankfully, my husband agreed. If you are married or have a significant other, it is more than important to have their agreement on any of these ideas. Either they are going to help you or at least be your support team member or not. If they are not at least on the same page as you about it, you are fighting an uphill battle and it makes your success difficult. Not necessarily impossible, but difficult.

The idea took off like a rocket and turned into a full time money making business for my husband.

I look back on how many times the idea had crossed my mind. I don't know if it would have taken off as well 20 years ago as the economy was so good.

The area where I reside has also grown considerably in 20 years thus adding more homes to the area.

People also seem to have less time than they did 20 years ago. This factor is something that may help you generate money with several of the ideas I've outlined.

I write as though I'm talking with you across the kitchen table. I also try to include examples or experiences if possible as this is not a text book type read.

Most likely, if you're reading this book, you are looking for a way to make extra money. You may not have computer skills or you may be a high level programmer without income coming in.

You may be in your 20's or you may be in your 80's. It really doesn't matter what your age is or if you can type or have a computer. These ideas are ones that almost anyone can use to make money.

Scrapping/Junking

There are plenty of finds in other people's trash.

You've probably heard the saying – one man's trash is another man's treasure. This is definitely the case.

The price of scrap metal has fallen considerably from a high of a couple hundred to a current price of around fifty dollars a ton but there is still money to be made.

Other metals such as aluminum and copper have different prices. The rates may vary per scrapyard and it is worth calling each one if you have several in your area.

You may find that you take scrap metal to one yard and aluminum to another to get the best payouts. Don't be pound wise and penny foolish.

In other words, if one yard is one cent less a pound, but they are twenty miles further away than the other yard, it may be best to go to the closest yard.

You'll also need a place to store your metal temporarily.

If you are on the lookout for other things such as items to sell at a flea market, eBay, garage sale etc. you may need to store them for a longer period.

You also may need to be able to mend or repair items that you plan on reselling.

You will need a vehicle and money for gas.

I have seen people on bikes and even walking in their neighborhoods.

Depending on what you are looking for, sometimes walking the neighborhood can be just as profitable as driving around neighborhoods.

Be sure to check with your city/town to make sure scrapping is allowed. Some cities/towns do require a permit. Some do not allow scrapping at all.

Make sure the item is truly out on the curb for trash pickup. Up by the house doesn't count.

A mower on the parkway may be there because the homeowner is taking a break not because he is throwing away his mower.

Never, ever dig through someone's garbage. If an item is in a box, take the box with you, don't leave a mess behind.

Don't fully disregard the idea of scrapping/junking if it doesn't appeal to you immediately.

You'll see that scrapping/junking can be useful with other money making strategies later in this book.

Flipping Cars

A friend of mine who resides in another state has paid his bills for years by flipping two cars a month on average.

He leans towards cars that he can re-sell fast for 5k and up and most of his cars are bought for 2500 and up.

He then has them detailed and has a mechanic who works on them. As he brings the mechanic at least two cars each month, he has a special rate arrangement.

I will also add that he has a pretty nice lifestyle. He drives a late model luxury car and has a set strategy each day. He works this job as a business not a side job.

But what if you don't have 5k or 2k to put into a car? If you have mechanical ability or have a friend who does, you still can make money flipping cars. Don't get in over your head though.

I've personally picked up several cars from people who bought the cars at auto auctions or other places and bit off way more than they could chew. I've also walked away from cars such as these where a person was green and paid too much.

You need to know your repair costs and be certain of those costs. If you buy a car and you are wrong in being able to fix it, you need to be able to get your money back on the car by selling the car to the scrapyard.

If scrap is at fifty dollars a ton or two hundred dollar a ton, you still need to have a way to get the car to the scrap yard.

The per ton rate is before tires are deducted, coolant is deducted, non- metal parts are deducted etc. I've watched people collect the money at the pay window at the scrap yard and then become very upset because they didn't ask questions beforehand.

The per ton is not the per ton of the entire vehicle but the per ton of the parts of the car that the scrap yard will accept. You also must have a title for the vehicle in most cases. Policies vary per scrapyard so check in advance.

If you buy a car for 300-400 and it needs some minor mechanical work that you or a friend can handle, then yes, you can flip that car for 1000 or maybe even more.

There is good money to be made and some vehicles have seasonal rate increases such as 4WD in snowy winter weather. The months around tax time – late January to April in this area- also bring an increase in car buyers and a decrease in people wanting to haggle over prices.

Be sure when you sell a car that you give the person a bill of sale.

You can find a template online or at your local library but the main thing is to list the car details – make, model, year, VIN, selling price and to write that the car is being sold as is.

Have two copies – you and the buyer will sign and date both copies and then you will keep one and give the other copy to the buyer.

I also make a copy of the title and attach it to my paperwork.

Lessons learned –

Different vehicles sell better in different areas.

This area – the Midwest – does well with Jeep Cherokees. My friend mentioned earlier flips Mercedes easily – go figure. Once you find the best vehicles, you can cherry pick your vehicles.

Another lesson – buyer beware on titles.

Examine all titles closely before buying.

We went to see a car over three hours away with a supposedly clean title. I looked at the title and upon very close inspection saw that it was a duplicate title and clearly stated that there may be a lien on the vehicle, this was a duplicate title.

There is a huge difference between getting a replacement title because a title was lost and getting a duplicate title of a vehicle that has a lien or it. Don't ever feel rushed. Study the title, ask questions and walk away if something doesn't seem right.

Salvage titled vehicles are ones we avoid.

Vehicles with rebuilt titles are ones I would also avoid.

We bought a bought a vehicle with a rebuilt title. It needed mechanical work which was done at no additional cost as my husband has mechanical abilities. We bought it extremely cheap, and as a test.

Thus far – zero bites on it. The vehicle is very clean inside and outside is in good condition. I am certain the title is the problem.

Hindsight being foresight – would I have bought that vehicle if I knew then what I know now? The answer is a resounding No!

At this point, I am not in a hurry to sell it so we can sit on it for awhile.

We bought it for so little money that even with scrap being low we can, at the least, reak even.

 Worst case, we can use it ourselves but then you have to think about license plate and insurance costs.

Another lesson – if it sounds too good to be true, it probably is. Be careful, never, ever wire money to anyone to hold a vehicle or buy a vehicle sight unseen. Odds are high you will never see your money again or the vehicle.

If a vehicle needs repair, be certain, very certain, of the repair costs. Look at vehicle cost, repair cost, selling cost.

We bought a lovely SUV two years ago. It needed, and still needs, an engine.

When you buy a vehicle that needs work, you need to know the current scrap prices. This way worst case scenario, you can haul it to be scrapped and at the least break even. With scrap currently being low, you need to be extra cautious with vehicles needing repair.

The SUV I just mentioned – we bought it with the calculation of scrap being at almost 200 a ton, so I knew at worst, we could take it to the scrap yard and at the least, break even.

Unfortunately, several things happened shortly thereafter, my husband discovered that this was the one year for this SUV that engines were in very short supply and extremely high priced. So we let it sit in the garage, watching for a used engine.

Then my husband fell ill and was hospitalized. He was unable to do any mechanical work for months, we had medical bills to deal with and no extra cash to put in an engine, even if we could find one. Plus even if we had an engine free, my husband couldn't lift to put it in.

Then – the final straw. Scrap metal prices fell and fell and fell.

We took another car in to be scrapped and went back the very same day to see metal had dropped 20 more dollars a ton from that morning.

So now we have a very expensive paperweight in the garage as we are beyond upside down on it. Our current thought is parting it out which takes us to the next idea coming up soon.

Last lesson learned – remember to write on the bill of sale that the vehicle is being sold as is. I include a sentence that states that the buyer has examined the – insert vehicle name- and understands that it is being sold as is, there is no guarantee and no refund.

Fortunately we have done this on every vehicle sold. One was a problem afterwards. The car was sold to a guy who then raced it and blew the engine. Later we found out that this wasn't the first time this had happened. About a month later he called and wanted his money back, claiming the engine was blown. Unfortunately, he and his father did not grasp that this was their problem not ours. The father made some rather nasty threats, including that he knew where we lived, and upon stating that we were reporting them both to the local police, that was the end of that matter.

We found out later that the guy had raced the car and done damage to the car which he had also done to his previous car.

Having the signed document was important.

You also may want to consider meeting people at a parking lot, in daytime. This is what my friend does who flips cars.

Never, ever agree to meet someone late at night.

If you are going to buy a car and the person wants you to meet them late at night, pass on that vehicle.

We do not tell the seller what we are driving and we always drive by the house where the vehicle is before pulling up.

There are criminals who prey on people – so always use care and always take someone with you when you are going to buy or sell a vehicle.

Selling Vehicle Parts

If you have a vehicle that doesn't run or isn't worth repairing, check online such as on Craigslist to see what parts sell for.

You may be extremely surprised to see that by parting it out you can get more than you would selling the whole car intact.

We've benefitted a few times from this strategy – here is one example-

We bought two cars – one to use for the engine and the other one needed an engine.

We then parted out the one car after the engine was pulled.

It is a time consuming business but we covered the costs of both cars with parting out the one and had scrap left over that brought in another couple hundred.

Just remember to make a list, take great photos and know when to stop parting out and haul away the remains to be scrapped.

Flipping Lawn Mowers and Snow Blowers

I know three people who make very good money flipping lawn mowers and snow blowers.

Again, you will in most cases need to have some basic mechanical ability to tune up the machines.

Many times you may be able to find the machines while scrapping so your only cost is gas money for scrapping.

In many cases, a mower or snow blower may just need a simple tune up.

I definitely advise picking up the junkers too as often you can salvage parts.

Make sure the mower or snow blower is well cleaned and is ready to go to work before you sell it.

The metal parts that are not salvageable or worth saving can be added to your scrap pile – see the section on Scrapping/Junking.

You can list your machines on sites such as Craigslist.

Make sure you include photos that really showcase the machine.

You can also take the machines to your local flea market to sell or re-sell to someone who sells at the flea market.

Seasonal Lawn Work

People will pay you to mow their lawn, rake their leaves, remove their snow etc.

You may be thinking yes, but there are a ton of lawn care/snow removal companies in the town where I live already.

I can tell you first hand as my husband owns a profitable lawn care/snow removal company – there are more people needing jobs done than there are companies to do them.

Also – many people just need a one- time mow when they are on vacation or people get injured and can't do the lawn work or snow removal for several weeks.

Lawn care companies usually will not take the one time client as it is not cost effective.

If there is a very large snow storm, people who did not contract with a snow removal company before the cold weather season are often out of luck unless they can find someone like you.

Persistence does pay off when it comes to getting regular customers.

Going door to door is not something that I recommend.

Creating a flyer and distributing it so that you are building an awareness of your service, is one way to advertise.

Know the going rates and don't underprice yourself. Underpricing does not necessarily mean value to people, especially with lawn care and snow removal.

Handyman work

I ran an ad to see if there was an interest for a handyman in the city where I live.

It was amazing to me how many people called.

The projects are usually small – hanging blinds, taking down blinds, removing brush – the list goes on.

Moving appliances out to the curb and picking up furniture, including mattresses, from stores was another popular request.

Think mainly small, quick jobs that need a helping hand.

You can create flyers and distribute them locally. Senior citizen centers are a good starting place. If you have senior citizen communities that is another good area to distribute flyers.

You may want to contact local visiting nurse and hospice groups to let them know about your service.

Check with your town beforehand to see if you need to register or get a permit to hand out flyers.

If you are called to haul appliances or hot water heaters out to the curb, let the caller know that you do free haul away.

You then can take the appliance to the scrap yard to add a few extra dollars to what you charge.

Swimming pool take down and haul away is another project that may generate at least a few calls in the spring or fall.

Oil changes and simple auto repair and maintenance

This can also fall under handyman work – please see the section on handyman projects- but you can also specialize in just doing oil changes and basic car repair/maintenance.

If you have smaller mom and pop gas stations in your town, get to know the owner and ask if you can leave flyers or cards outlining your mechanical services.

If someone pulls up with a flat tire and you can repair tires, the gas station may be more than happy to give the person your phone number.

Small car dealerships also may be interested in your service.

Once you start offering oil changes you may be pleasantly surprised regarding the amount of business that you will build.

If you go to a commercial oil change place, you often have to wait an hour or so. You are also upsold a variety of products and services making a 20 dollar oil change an 80 dollar oil change. I can tell you this from personal experience.

If you pick up a car for a client while he/she is at work or on the weekend, and then handle the oil change and return the vehicle, they have saved themselves the wait time and also saved themselves from being pitched a variety of upsell and services.

If you offer your service to hospital or other large companies, word of mouth will quickly spread and you may find yourself doing oil changes all day.

You can also offer simple maintenance services such as changing windshield wiper blades, making sure windshield wiper fluid is full etc.

These small projects are ones that many people simply cannot get done especially if they work.

There is nothing worse than a long day at work and then being tired and having to wait at an oil change place or commuting home after a long day at work to find out that you are out of windshield wiper fluid and not even halfway home.

Car washing and auto detailing

Car detailing at a dealership or commercial car wash is often quite expensive.

Plus, after work or on the weekend, many people simply do not have the time to take their car in for detailing.

Once word gets about the quality service that you provide, you'll begin seeing referrals and also word of mouth clients.

With all services, from lawn care to auto repair and everything in between, offering a referral compensation, often generates additional business.

When you begin consider placing flyers and business cards around town, especially if you have senior citizen programs in town or a hospital or office complex.

You want to go where as many people as possible will see your flyer or business cards.

Grocery stores with bulletin boards are another resource.

Craigslist is an option also but use care and set your parameters a far as location. You aren't going to want customers that are an hour away.

You also need to make sure you follow any zoning ordinances in your town. If you are renting a home or apartment, most likely you will not be able to wash cars and detail them at home.

However, you can take the car to a commercial do it yourself car wash and possible even do your detailing there too.

If you own your own home, you may be able to wash/detail cars at home depending upon the volume and also upon your neighbors.

Pick up and Deliveries

While this could fall under handyman service, you can develop a great niche just on local deliveries and haul–aways.

Many of the big box/discount/wholesale stores do not offer delivery.

Even though my husband has a lawn care company, we receive a steady amount of calls asking if we do furniture and appliance delivery.

The first few times I found this strange as we do not advertise anything but lawn care and snow removal.

We used to do garage clean outs but it was by word of mouth several years ago. We do not advertise this service and haven't done it for at least three full years.

He has done pick up – furniture and appliances - for a couple lawn care clients and there is definitely room in our area to expand this idea.

While it may not be a full time job, this could be a good weekend cash flow.

The moving of furniture and other belongings is also a related niche.

www.HireaHelper.com offers consumers the ability to locate moving help via their site. UHaul used to have a similar set up a few years ago as I used contractors twice via a link that I know I found via the UHaul site but I did not find it when I searched today so it may no longer be in business.

You can look into posting on freelance sites like the ones mentioned, post local ads in your grocery store and also consider posting on www.Craigslist.com

Ideally, you should have your own trailer but you can also rent trucks and trailers from places like UHaul or Enterprise and factor the expense into your quote. If you become a regular renter, ask the company if they offer discounts or have special promotions.

Enterprise is very good at rewarding repeat customers.

Foreclosure clean outs/Estate clean outs

There is very good money in foreclosure clean outs.

My husband met a local guy who now has a crew that helps him clean out foreclosures.

He gets to keep all the contents in the home but he also has the expense of a dumpster and removing any garbage and debris.

Many foreclosures end up being stripped almost bare but in some cases people leave appliances, furniture and other household items.

You may also be able to negotiate a cleaning fee or, at the least, get the dumpster paid for.

Be prepared to dress to protect yourself from any mold spores and remember that if it is winter, the furnace will not be operational in the home so dress accordingly.

Items that you end up with can be sold.

For example- junk or broken items that are metal can be sold to the scrap yard.

Furniture can be sold on Craigslist, eBay or at a flea market.

If you donate items to Goodwill, get a slip showing your donations for a tax deduction.

Contact your local banks to inquire what the process is to be considered for foreclosure clean outs.

With estate clean outs, a family may have relatives in another town who have gone into a nursing home or passed away.

Before the house can be listed to sell, it will need to be cleaned out. You can place an ad, such as on Craigslist.com but I also suggest contacting local real estate offices and ask if they are working with someone regarding clean outs.

 If so, still ask if you may leave your flyer or card with them. You never know as companies may decide to give someone else a shot.

Local Taxi

Often senior citizens and others may need a way to get to the store or doctor's office.

Other people may need a way to get to work, especially in cold weather if their car won't start.

If there is not a taxi service in your area, their options may be limited.

Being able to take people to the store or on errands may be a valuable service that brings repeat business.

If you live a distance from large airports, taking someone to and from the airport can also be a lucrative money maker.

My husband has two friends in the local taxi business.

One caters mainly to senior citizens. He drives a mini -van. It is not a newer model but he does keep it very clean and well maintained.

The other friend is one of several in his family who takes people to and from the airport. They often have more work than they can handle as they have tried to entice my husband in to helping them numerous times.

I know that limo service from this area to the airport an hour and a half away exceeds one hundred twenty five dollar, plus a tip, for a shared limo going one way.

Logically, you can offer your service for less but don't underprice your services.

Paper delivery

Newspaper delivery is an option that I recently looked into after seeing several ads in the local grocery store.

While it may not be as fast cash-wise and most likely you will be taxed on your income, I am including it as it is a lucrative income opportunity that many people do not think about.

I think it can be a good income stream for the right person and I met many dedicated and hardworking people who deliver the local newspapers in this area.

The benefit is that it is a daily and consistent work flow.

The schedule may be a benefit depending on if you are a night owl.

While each newspaper will have a different routine and pay schedule, following is an overview of what I found when I looked into being a newspaper carrier in my area.

You need a reliable vehicle that has room for a good volume of papers and is gas efficient.

You will need a good flashlight and probably a larger handheld light such as a spotlight.

 If possible, I suggest having a helper.

You will need to pick up the papers from a location and in some cases, you will need to put the papers in plastic sleeves.

I suggest plastic totes or some type of crate to contain the papers.

You will have a print out of street addresses and the list may change daily or have additions. The winter holiday season will be a heavier workload as more people subscribe to get a paper with sale ads in November and December.

Stores also do more marketing and may contract with local newspapers to deliver catalogs and/or inserts to not only newspaper subscribers but also non- subscribers.

Check with your tax professional but if you are classified as independent contractor, you may be able to deduct mileage and gas expenses. I suggest checking beforehand so you are documenting properly for tax deductions.

Flea Market Selling

Several years ago, while visiting a local flea market, my husband and I had the same idea at just about the same time.

That idea evolved into having three booths and people who sold our merchandise on a commission basis.

I ended up writing a book on our flea market success as well as publishing a USA based wholesale directory.

The nice thing about selling at a flea market is the flexibility. Most flea markets are open on the weekends and many people make more in a few hours on the weekend than they ever made working a forty hour job.

Outside space generally is less money and often paid on an as used arrangement. Indoor space is generally a monthly rental but in many cases, you can leave your merchandise there versus having to pack up.

You also are not at the effects of the weather.

I love flea market selling for many reasons – the time put in versus money made, the flexibility and the people are just three reasons.

You may be wondering about inventory. You can start with items in your home and/or offer to sell items for family/friends on a commission basis.

This is also an area where scrapping/junking pays off as you may be able to sell items that you have found while scrapping/junking.

If you are scrapping/junking and come across lamps on a regular basis, you may be able to take one without a shade and pair it with a shade from another lamp that is damaged.

Depending upon the area where you live, you can in many cases, find new or like new items parked on the curb. These are perfect for selling at the flea market.

eBay selling

I think we've all heard about the eBay super sellers who make fistfuls of dollars daily.

My sister in law is very successful on eBay.

I have tried, very hard, to get enthused about the idea of selling on eBay.

It is just no something that would fit into my daily schedule as you need to have time to do the following-

Find the items

Make sure the items are clean and in selling condition

Take photos

Create a listing

Package the item

Ship the item

Do any customer service that may be needed

This is a 7 day a week job. As mentioned my sister in law is very successful on eBay. I know it is not for me but it may be something of interest to you, just go in to it with the understanding that it is time consuming. You do of course need a computer if eBay interests you.

Here's a shortcut – eBay sellers. These are people who will sell your items on eBay for you. They do all the work – the research, the listing, the photos, the collection of funds, the shipping and the customer service.

In return, they take a commission from the items that they sell for you.

There was a seller in a neighboring town but they had closed their doors recently which I found out when I was researching ideas for this book.

With that being said, if you utilize a seller, find out what their policy is if they decide to close. Also ensure you have photos and details on every item that you give them to sell.

Arrowheads and other cool things to sell

From selling at the flea market and having a brother who collects them, I found out that arrowheads sell like crazy in this area. There is not a weekend that goes by at the flea market that someone doesn't stop by our booths and ask if we have arrowheads or know someone who does.

You may find something else to sell besides arrowheads but my point is, there are many cool things that people will pay instant cash for.

LP records are another big seller in this area.

Certain glassware, tools, arrowheads – there is an endless amount of ideas.

You can sell at flea markets or online. You may have a consignment shop in town that will take your items too.

The main thing is to take a look at what you may have on hand or be able to get that other people will give you fast cash for.

If you pair this idea with one of the other ideas such as foreclosure clean outs you may have a very good inventory of merchandise to sell on eBay, online or at flea markets.

We netted over 100 popular movies in DVD form a couple years ago. It was part of a haul away project at a home that had been put up for sale in a high end neighborhood. That project also brought bags of name brand clothing that was like new, American Girl merchandise, an Xbox and two handheld game systems. Along with those treasures there was boxes of like new high end holiday decorations and bedding. The owners had left the merchandise. I think perhaps the home was in foreclosure – usually you aren't given details. We ended up with our front room packed wall to wall. We pitched about 20 percent and the rest was sold at the flea market. The clothing we gave to my sister in law to sell on eBay.

House Cleaning

Franchise cleaning services charge a good amount of money to clean homes.

They are also licensed and bonded so please keep that in mind as you may be asked if you are too.

I found out through our insurance agent that you can get a million dollar liability policy for a surprisingly low cost. Being bonded is not a high investment either.

House cleaning opportunities may vary from someone laid up by a sprained ankle to a busy person who commutes to a senior citizen who just can't get the job done.

You will need to bring your own supplies but you can also see if the person wants you to use theirs – such as they use a specific brand. If so, be sure to reduce your price.

I suggest a flat rate per room. Some rooms will be more, some less. You can discount the rate, such as doing a third bedroom at a discounted rate.

The first cleaning may be higher priced especially if the home hasn't been cleaned in a while.

If you use an hourly rate, people will expect you to move faster as they want to pay as little as possible.

Having a flat rate helps you as you don't feel rushed and it helps your client as they know the expense beforehand.

Garage/Basement Cleaning

This is a bit different than house cleaning as it may be a one-time service. However, it also has some good perks.

Usually, once Spring arrives people start cleaning out their garages. There are people who accumulate so much stuff that their garage is beyond packed full.

Sometimes the amount of work to clean it out is overwhelming. Other times, the homeowner just doesn't have the time.

If a person is moving or planning on putting their home on the market, they know they have a certain time limit in which to get this project done.

The first thing that you need to determine with your potential client is – how much of the stuff is going to be tossed out? Then you need to think about how much of the stuff to be thrown out that you can move be it to the scrap yard or to sell or to use yourself.

Do not discard anything other than pure rubbish without thinking about options. Tires, for example, are often passed by and dumped yet tires with a good tread can often be resold at a flea market, online or in some cases sold to local tire stores who sell used tires to customers. These are the smaller, independent tire stores often in ethnic areas.

Used appliances can also be sold. With scrap prices down, working appliances can be sold online or at flea markets. As with used tires, you may be able to find a store that sells used appliances who will buy the appliances from you.

Old car parts, such as brakes, can be taken to the scrap yard and sold.

So take a good look at what the client wants cleaned out. Do you need a dumpster for the rubbish or can you make do with bagging into contractor or heavy garbage bags?

I think you know this, but you are not going to share with the client what you are doing with the items. If you are able to resell the items or scrap them, that is your business.

You are being paid to clean out their garage or basement. What you do with the merchandise is up to you. The only exception to this is, if you come across something that may have obvious sentimental value to the owner or family, I do suggest asking them if they would like to keep it.

If you come across tax returns, bank statements and things of that nature, I would give these to the owner or family also.

If the clean out is one that will take more than a day and is detailed in nature, I highly suggest having a written agreement that both parties sign.

Lesson learned -

My husband did a haul away in which the homeowner was remodeling a house and garage to flip.

The agreement was to haul away all the old wood and concrete. In exchange, my husband was to take a large quantity of metal. Metal was at 200 a ton so this was a very good arrangement.

There was a lot more debris than we had been told over the phone but we still figured we had a good amount of metal to cash in.

The individual was insistent that he take the non-metal first, which made sense. The dump that the guy told him to go to was closed and had been closed for years. In hindsight, this was our first red flag.

By the time we located a different dump, drove there and unloaded, we had lost about two hours of time.

Upon returning to the home, the gates were closed and the homeowner didn't answer his mobile. He had stated earlier he had to go to work in the afternoon so we thought that was what had happened.

We then called and went back to the home daily for a few days. He never answered his phone. Over a week passed. We had called and drove by several times and finally, one day, the gate was open.

My husband went to the door and it was evident the guy was taken back by our persistence. He tried saying we never came back or called and my husband told him we had phone records showing numerous calls and yes, we had drove by several times and the gates were closed.

The guy then stated he had gave the metal to someone else.

He finally offered twenty five dollars to my husband for his gas money. Needless to say, this was ridiculous but we learned our lesson the hard way.

In hindsight, I think he planned the whole thing out in advance, sending us on a wild goose chase to a long closed dump. We should have checked beforehand regarding dumps and options.

Make sure you have a signed agreement listing your compensation and the arrangement.

Garage Sales – Having and Attending

I'll be the first to say – I'm not fond of having garage sales. They are not something that you should throw up overnight, they need a lot of planning and time to organize.

 But…….they are a way to generate cash fast and within a couple hours.

My tips – organize, organize, organize.

Be sure that you know the best day in your town for garage sales and the best time range.

Know the going prices for items and be willing to accept offers and sell box lots of things.

I go to a good amount of garage sales and being bunt, I've only seen one or two that are as organized as mine are.

My organization and marketing pays off though as when I've had garage sales almost everything sells including the items used for makeshift tables.

Be sure to have plenty of plastic bags, paper for wrapping and change on hand.

Be ready to cut your prices as the time to close nears and also give box deals. For example, I saw a woman looking at a used sewing machine and a box of tapes. She then asked the price on the sewing machine was negotiable. It was about an hour before closing. I replied that she could have the machine and box of tapes for the current price on the sewing machine.

Another lady was looking at curtains from my daughter's room and I bundled the pillow shams in which were still new in the bag if she took both.

People love getting deals and I like creating deals that make them smile.

If you have toys or children's books, keep a box by you and offer one to each child, with the parent's agreement, when the parent is paying for their items.

Greet each visitor. I am surprised when I go to a garage sale and am basically ignored by the person holding the sale. You don't have to be chummy but at least say hello and let them know if they have questions or need help, just to let you know.

Be prepared to offer bulk prices. My husband noticed a box full of used car stereos at one garage sale. No prices – just a box full on a table. Remember, we flip cars and have a flea market so this is a goldmine example.

He asked the prices and finally the woman came up with two prices based on the brands. He then asked for a price to take the entire box. The time it took to get the initial pricing and box pricing was way too long.

If you have a box full of something, be prepared if someone comes in and asks how much for all of it?

Her price was fair but you can also counter offer when you are at a garage sale, just put yourself in their shoes too.

Some garage sales you will see that there is no sense in counter offering as the prices are just insane. Make sure if you have a garage sale that your prices are realistic but also do your research so you don't give away the farm.

I have bought name brands such as a Prada purse and an Ed Hardy purse (brand new with tags still on) for 3 dollars each, buried in huge boxes filled with purses, totes and shoes.

Yes, I could re-sell both but decided to keep both as they were both my type of style and really, how could I not keep them? Every time I look at them, they remind me of the value of digging in boxes at garage sales.

Had the garage sale holder had these two purses on a table and nicely displayed they could have made a lot more money and still had fast sales.

At another garage sale, in late autumn, I bought two men's polo shirts, designer brand for 2 dollars each, tags still on. Had it been spring or summer, she could have gone up a couple dollars but she was smart in a lower price due to the season.

I know of a woman in a neighboring town who scraps/junks and then takes her finds home and has a weekly garage sale.

She came to my attention as when on our way to do a garage clean out, I saw this beautiful mirror sitting curbside in someone's garbage. My husband saw my interest and said after we did the garage clean out, we could pick up the mirror.

The look on my face was what he already knew – that mirror would be long gone. So less than a quarter block later, we turned around to go back for the mirror. It was gone.

Not even five minutes and gone.

My husband knew how much I liked the mirror but I never said any more about it as, well, what good would it do, it was already gone.

The next morning, my husband left our home unusually early saying he was just running an errand.

About an hour later he was back, trying to hide something quite large behind him. It was the mirror.

He went back to the subdivision on a hunch and drove around the area where the mirror was. Seeing a garage sale, he stopped. There was my mirror, with a 40 dollar price tag.

He haggled to no avail and the point blank told her the story about how we passed it by and turned around. It still cost him 25 but he was determined to bring the mirror home.

He said that he thought about it that night, how the mirror was grabbed up so quickly and the more he thought about it, he felt the mirror was in that same area and sure enough it was.

The woman was making a fairly tidy profit weekly and anything she didn't sell she just tried to sell again the next week.

If you are home on the day that garage sales are most popular in your area – here it is on Thursdays- this may be a lucrative money maker for you.

Dog Treats

This one may cause you to do a double take or not. The pet industry has grown substantially the past few years. Pet stores and boutiques are popping up everywhere.

The latest trend that has swept the pet industry and stuck is organic and raw food diets for pets.

Pet boutiques and pet stores are offering dog treats, bakery style. The treats are in glass cases. Some are the traditional dog bone style but the flavors may vary from bacon to pumpkin to sweet potato.

Others may look like cookies with ones like fire hydrants, dogs, bones etc.

Others may look like donuts.

The ideas are endless and the profit margins are there.

You will need to do your research regarding selling to boutiques. You may need a business license, you may need a license, you may need insurance.

You will of course need excellent recipes and the ability to make professional looking treats that dogs love.

This is not an idea that would reap instant, fast cash but it is one that could turn into a profitable business with a very low start up.

Farmer's Markets

This is a great money making idea once you determine what sells.

While this idea may not bring in as much money as other ideas, you may be able to turn a handful of seeds into seedlings and turn a tidy profit.

I have a neighbor who crafts beautiful hand painted bird houses in the winter and sells them at farmer's markets in the warm months.

Most farmer's markets are half day events scheduled weekly. Usually May through October.

I've seen plants, garden vegetables and fruits, honey and more.

The other things that I've seen is where this idea gets interesting –

Homemade soaps – you know the type. The beautiful slabs of soap that are sliced. These can also be sold to local boutiques.

Cheese and bread – I came across two different vendors at a local farmer's market. One sold bread and the other cheese. They both were always swarming with customers. The lines for both stretched farther than all the other vendor's lines combined. People loved the idea of buying the bread and cheese at the farmer's market.

Upon a closer look, which then resulted in a second visit to confirm what I thought that I saw, I determined the bread vendor was not baking his own bread and selling it. They were buying artisan bread from a Chicago bakery and repackaging it. It is a husband and wife team. They are lovely people. They dress in a nice Bohemian style clothing mix and play their roles well. You would never know this wasn't their own baked bread. In Chicago, there are sections in the city that sell produce and other food at wholesale to restaurants and others. They are buying the bread in limited quantities and then repackage in a plain clear plastic bag. Had I not noticed something in their booth, I never, ever would have guessed their secret.

With that observation in mind, I paid closer attention to the cheese vendor. Baking bread at home is a project but cheese, well, cheese is something that needs a lot more time and effort than bread. The vendor had quite the assortment of cheese versus just one or two. Upon closer observation, I am more than certain that they too, are repackaging.

The soap sellers, one I was fairly certain made her own and the other, well, I just wasn't sure.

I just came across a wholesale soap seller when updating my USA wholesale directory and their soap looked home -made.

Is repackaging wrong?

That is a tough question as I think it depends upon each individual.

However, depending upon your town and county, it also may be looked at differently too.

I was at an indoor traveling flea market and watched the county sheriff come in accompanied by someone from the Board of Health.

A bread seller was shut down on the spot as he did not have a permit from the county by the Board of Health. He tried arguing that his bread was sealed by the manufacturer – he hadn't repackaged it. They still would not let him sell the bread.

So definitely do your research before selling any food items. Ordinances and permits vary by town and county. I would also look into insurance if selling food products.

I think dog treats would also sell well at many farmer's markets. This is another product that I definitely advise checking with the farmer's market about permits and then also checking into insurance.

Dog Walker/Pet Sitter

Take a close look in your neighborhood and you may be surprised to see how many people are walking their dogs.

The challenge is Mr. Dog is often left home all day while his owner works, especially if you live in an area with a high amount of commuters.

If you have a large park or county fairgrounds, offering a daily walk in town and also a longer walk session to parks etc. may be a welcome service for dog owners.

Pet sitting is another service that is growing in demand.

This service may vary from stopping in at a client's home in the morning, afternoon and evening to feed a pet while his/her owner is away on the weekend to staying with a pet while his/her owner is on vacation.

Dog Bather

While this alone is not a fast cash, high money maker, it is a service that can be added to handyman services or dog walker services.

Dog bathing is not dog grooming.

You need to be clear about this to your clients. You also need to find out the rates in your area that dog groomers charge for dog bathing.

This service helps people who may not have the time to take their dog to be bathed.

Many of the larger pet stores offer a self -serve dog wash.

The local pet store in my town offers a self -serve dog wash for 10 dollars a wash.

Around the Christmas holiday they offer a discounted package that is good all year. You can purchase a card that makes the wash 5.00 each versus 10.00 dollars

They provide the shampoo, towels and dryer in private rooms.

This is nice as you may have one dog who needs oatmeal soap, one who needs flea soap etc.

If the dog needs grooming, you may want to consider offering your dog walking clients a service in which you take their dog to and from the dog groomer. This may only be a charge of a few dollars but it will be a good way to stand out as a dog walker.

Sewing and Alterations

In the town where I live, since I was maybe twelve years old, all of my clothes have been altered by a Polish lady who attended the same church.

Freshly arrived from Poland, she began in a small building in town. She spoke very little English at that time but her sewing and alteration abilities were stellar. Word quickly grew and she added staff.

She became a much loved and recognized person in the area.

Prom time – you needed to have your dress in to her a good month in advance.

Broken zipper on your winter coat? Good as new and back to you within the week.

Interestingly enough, no competition sprang up and forty years later, she retired and went back to Poland. The shop was closed. No one has stepped up to take her place or at least try to.

I have zero sewing ability and I have a growing pile of my husband's work jackets with rips, tears and broken zippers.

Do you sew? You may be able to do alterations out of your home. Check with local dry cleaners and see if they would be interested in offering your service for a percentage of sales.

You also may want to advertise in your town's newspaper or your church bulletin.

Lessons

Do you have skill that may be of interest of others to learn? Skills such as golfing and musical ability come to mind.

You may have already thought of another skill.

People are interested in learning.

Being accomplished on the piano (or other musical instrument) or golf course is marketable and people may be willing to pay for your time so that they too can learn.

My daughter took guitar lessons for years. My husband recently took drum lessons. Both instructors worked full time day jobs and gave lessons in the evening or on the weekend.

If you have a skill and are interested in giving lessons, this idea may be worth considering.

There are many ways to make money, and in a lot of cases, it is fast cash paid out, often that day.

Some of the ideas that I've shared with you may be ones that you've already thought of before.

I was a bit hesitant when we started the flea market business but when after a couple hours on a Sunday I was making more than many people made working a forty hour week, I was glad we gave the idea a go. When week after week we saw money come in after just a few hours on a Sunday, we realized the huge potential and we also realized we were having fun.

I like the freedom of implementing ideas like these. Yes, you need to work them and consider them a job but it is wonderful being your own boss. With many of these ideas, you also meet some really nice people.

Many of these ideas can be done after work or on weekends.

If you don't have a job, you may be able to create multiple cash streams by implementing several of these ideas.

You may also create your own unique idea after reading my ideas. Maybe instead of arrowheads you realize that there is a very good market for selling baseball cards in your area. Or doing carpet cleaning or rototilling. Each area is different – look around and see what niche is popular and what you could do to make money.

Money is all around us, sometimes we just need to look at the world a bit differently to see this is true.

Sometimes you just get to the point where if others don't see your value as an employee, you can create your own wealth and be your own boss.

Thank you for taking the time to read through this book. I hope that you have found some ideas that are useful and that you are soon generating cash daily from your implemented ideas.

Sincerely,

Diana

www.ingramcontent.com/pod-product-compliance
Lightning Source LLC
Chambersburg PA
CBHW051429200326
41520CB00023B/7406